Email Marketing Machine

Build Relationships, Get Traffic and Make Money Online

Argena Olivis

www.ArgenaOlivis.com

BONUS: Squeeze Page Traffic Machine Video + Bonus Report [FREE]

Get access to my newest course **Squeeze Page Traffic Machine** absolutely free. Learn how to drive targeted traffic to your squeeze using these simple tactics.

Visit <u>www.argenaolivis.com/squeezepagetraffic</u> for Access

Table of Contents

Introduction

Chapter 1: Establishing Your Target Market

Chapter 2: Creating Your Opt In Offer

Chapter 3: Getting Traffic to Your Squeeze Page

Chapter 4: Setting Up Auto Responders

Chapter 5: Selling

Chapter 6: Building Relationships

Conclusion

Introduction

I want to thank you and congratulate you for reading the book, *"Email Marketing Machine: Build Relationships Get Traffic and Make Money Online"*.

This book contains proven steps and strategies on how to get started with email marketing.

The importance of email is critical when in business, rather you own a brick and mortar or you have an online business; it's important to start building your email list to promote long-term relationships with customers in a secure way.

An email list is an asset that you turn to in the event that something goes wrong, you can use it to get in touch with your customers.

Email can also be used to make subscribers aware of promotions, coupons, new content, or anything else you want to share.

With just a click of a button, you can make a lot of money, add a lot of value, or make someone smile. Growing your list is critical if you want to create a loyal following.

The best thing about building a list is the security it gives you. Depending on your email marketing software, you'll have the ability download and or back up your list, and switch email software providers with ease.

If you want a secure line of communication between your audience and yourself, this is the recommended route to take; just ask any full-time internet marketer.

Your email list also an asset because it's a great way to sell without feeling bad or awkward. At any time of day, you can let subscribers know about your new products and services.

If you truly build relationships with your customers and give them what they want (lots of value), you can get to the point where you make instant sales by sending out a broadcast email about a new product you've created, or one that you're an affiliate for.

In *Email Marketing Machine*, you're going to discover how to establish your target market.

By knowing who your target market is, you are able to provide content and products for them that is relevant and useful.

You will also learn how to create an opt-in offer that will allow you to collect multiple email addresses with ease.

After that, you're going to learn how to get traffic to your squeeze page, and how to set up auto responders that help you to build relationships with your customers.

Then the fun part, you're going to learn how to sell to your list and how to build relationships so you can keep selling to them over and over again.

It's a win-win situation: Your subscribers are getting

tons of value in exchange for what they paid for or for

being a subscriber, and you'll get compensated for the

hard work you put in to make your subscribers happy

and educated on a subject.

Thanks again for reading *Email Marketing Machine*, I

know you'll enjoy the book if you take action so you can

see some results!

Associations.

Chapter 1: Establishing Your Target Market

How well do you know your customer? Do you know what they like to do? What their interests are? How can you help them? If not, that's okay we're going to learn all about that.

But first, you need to establish a niche if you haven't already. A niche is a specific topic that you want to focus on. You may already have a website, service, or product that already focuses on a specific topic.

There are some guidelines you need to follow when choosing your niche: profitability, knowledge, likeability, and size.

Profitability

Before you choose a niche, you want to ensure it's profitable. You can find this out by visiting Google.com and typing in your topic and seeing how other people are making money with this niche.

Visit a few of the top websites. If you choose this niche, these will be your competitors. Competition is a good thing, this means there's money to be made.

Don't worry too much about the size of their audience. The one thing that you can do differently is to be yourself. Your competitor can never be you, you're original so make sure to use that as an advantage. You shouldn't dwell on what you cannot change.

Also, make sure you have a mindset of abundance. Believe that there's enough to go around for everyone. If you're coming from a place where you're adding value and serving your audience, there's plenty of room for you and your business.

You have to have the right mindset to succeed in business. So work on your self-growth and confidence first if you've been at this for a while and still haven't taken action.

When you visit your competitor's website, look to see how they're making money. Do they offer coaching? Do they have a brick in mortar? Services? Their own store or products and courses? Affiliate marketing?

This most likely is how you will be making money too, so get some ideas and jot them down.

If the site you visit looks like they are making money with just advertising, you may want to stay away from that. Only because you don't want to put all your eggs in one basket.

If they have private ads from different companies, you may be onto something. But it's still too risky.

Do they have products or services in this niche? If they do, there's most likely people making money from it. This means it's profitable.

If you think about going into a niche that doesn't already

have products or services, this will not be a smart move.

Internet marketing has been around for years, and if no one has created a product for your niche, then it's most likely not profitable because it doesn't have a big enough audience.

You ultimately want to make a profit, and you can't do that with a non-profitable niche.

Other techniques you can use is to see if your niche has products on big sites like Clickbank or Amazon.com.

Use Amazon search to your advantage by seeing if there are at books selling on the topic you're thinking about getting into.

Do this by typing in a keyword and seeing how profitable the book is. You can tell how profitable a book is by the rank. If it's below 100,000 in the paid kindle store, this means it's making some money.

Knowledge

How much knowledge and experience do you have in the niche? You're going to need it.

You can always study a particular niche, but that's going to take a lot of time and be difficult for you.

But if you have the money, you can always outsource content using services such as Odesk, Elance, and Fiverr.

If you truly want to learn more about the niche, consider doing a "journey". This is where you take people through your journey of that niche.

For example: My site Argena Olivis is currently about my journey to online business success. I'm taking people on a journey and showing them how I'm creating multiple streams of income online.

You can do this with a niche too, but you truly have to be committed to learning a lot and growing over time so your audience can see progress.

You may be thinking that you can't find a niche because you're not necessarily good or passionate about anything in particular. Well, I think there has to be something you like a lot.

Think about how you spend your free time. Do you have any hobbies such as scrapbooking or fixing cars?

There's something you're good at. If you're truly struggling to find a niche, make sure to ask the people closest to you what they think you're good at and then try to find a profitable niche from there.

If you have a lot of money, and no time, consider outsourcing your content. This may be expensive, but it's totally worth it if you want to be in that niche.

You can do this by going to places like Fiver.com,

Odesk.com, and Elance.com.

Likeability

You have to like the niche you choose. If you don't like it, you're not going to stick with it and it's not fair to your audience.

You don't have to be passionate about it, but you should at least find it interesting.

It's dangerous getting into a niche you don't believe in or that you don't truly like. It will show through your emails and your content that you don't enjoy it.

If you don't truly like it, stay away from it. It's not worth the money if your stomach turns every time you have to create content.

Like I said, you don't have to be passionate, but you should come from a place of wanting to help others.

Size

Make sure you choose a niche that is not too small or too broad.

Small niches can be great because you have a very specific target market. But you have to look at it from a profitability standpoint too. Don't niche down so far that you're only talking to 20 people.

Don't have your niche so big that you're targeting everybody. This is a mistake. You can't please everyone so don't even try.

This will put a hindrance on building relationships, you can't build relationships through email if you're targeting every type of person.

Being able to stand out from the crowd also comes into play. You want to make sure you stand out and can differentiate yourself from the millions of business owners trying to make money online.

Example: You shouldn't create a market on general weight loss for everyone. Niche down and create a site for weight loss for women. Niche down even further and create a site for weight loss for women in college.

I wouldn't niche down any further than that, but this would be a good target market. Do you get my drift? You want to know who your target market is so you can actually find them and help them out.

This comes back to knowledge and experience, what do you know? How can being who you are, and where you are, be an advantage? Use that info to create your target market if it fits the guidelines.

If you get this part right and find a great target market, you'll make more money in the long run because you'll be able to connect with your audience better through your content and emails.

The Take Away

Please **do not skip this step** if you don't already have a target market! Without having a specific target market you won't know who to advertise to and who to create emails for.

Know your target market and what stage they're at in life. Are they a beginner or more advanced or anywhere in between?

Once you know who to market to, your life becomes easier and you're able to help other people solve their problems and make money doing it.

If you already have a target market that's great. If not, go through these steps and decide on one. You can always change it later, but for now, you want to get started.

I want you to get results from this book. So decide on your target, take action.

Chapter 2: Creating Your Opt-In Offer

An opt-in offer is a free product or service that you offer prospects in exchange for their email address.

Here are some examples of what you can offer prospects:

- eBook

- report

- chapter of a book

- guide

- checklist

- printables

- email course

- video course

- video

- free consultation

- audio

You want to give something of value away for free. The trick here is to give away something that your prospect would be willing to pay for.

But don't make the mistake of giving away too much too soon. This will overwhelm the prospect and they won't take action on anything you give them.

People don't value free stuff as much as they do paid stuff. So keep that in mind too.

You don't have to spend weeks on creating your opt-in offer, just create something of value and see if it's getting you email subscribers. If it's not, then you may one to change it or you may just need more traffic to your squeeze page.

Truthfully you can give away any freebie. You can even do a contest where you give away something and syour prospects would have to enter their name and email in order to win.

But if you want to automate your business so you can have time freedom, you may want to stick with a product that can be instantly delivered without you having to be involved.

Before you can do anything, you're going to need email

marketing software. I personally use Aweber, though there are free services you can use.

It depends on what your needs are. If you plan on selling to your list, keep in mind that many free services don't allow you to send out affiliate links.

You want to make sure you own a service that is your own, and if something happens you'll be able to get in touch with your list. Services like Aweber allow you to own your list, send affiliate links, and create opt-in pages and opt-in forms.

You can also export your list and save it just in case something happens you'll have a backup. A list is truly an asset so be careful what service you build it with.

There are also services like GetResponse and Infusionsoft. Whatever works best for you is great.

To learn more about setting up your list go to www.argenaolivis.com/email-marketing-101

Now we're going to go into how to create each opt-in offer.

eBook

eBook creation is pretty simple. All you're going to need is a service that allows you to create documents such as Microsoft Word, Open Office, or Pages for Mac.

Decide what your eBook will be about. Outline what you want to talk about and how long you want it to be.

An eBook can be as small as 5 pages but it's up to you. How long do you want it to be?

Once you finish deciding the topic, length, and outline of your eBook you're ready to begin typing.

Create your eBook and edit it. To increase opt-in rates you may want to create a cover for your book so your prospects can get a feel for what it looks like. A cover makes it look more valuable.

Once you're finished, export the document you've typed your eBook in as pdf. Then upload it into your media files in WordPress. Then get the link for the book and add it to the email auto-responder message that is sent immediately to your subscriber after they confirm their subscription.

You also have the option of having it delivered right after they confirm their subscription. Instead of having a thank you page, they can get access to the eBook right away.

But I like the first option better because they can have it in their email and refer back to it as they need it.

In that first email that is sent immediately after someone opts in, you can also add instructions on how to download it to their computer for future use. Also, let them know how they can get the best use out of it.

If you don't have a website, you can just make that first message that is sent to your email list immediately the eBook. This means your subscribers will have to read that entire first message as an "eBook". But it doesn't look as professional.

Report

Creating a report is basically has the same process as creating an eBook.

You want to create it in a document and export it as a pdf, and then upload it to your WordPress back office and put the link to it in the email that is sent immediately to your subscribers after they confirm their subscription.

The only difference is the report should be on a very specific topic and it can be much shorter than an eBook.

Chapter of A Book

If you have an eBook that you've written, and you don't want to give the whole thing away for free, consider giving the first chapter away to your email subscribers.

Deliver it in the same way you would deliver a report or an entire eBook.

This is really beneficial because you can presell a prospect on the book, and once they see what quality content you create you're more likely to sell more copies of your eBook.

Guide

A guide is similar to a report. It's specific and it shows someone how to do something specific.

Deliver it in the same way you would deliver a report or a chapter of an eBook. Guides are usually longer and more in depth. They usually consist of step by step instructions on how to do something.

Checklist

A checklist is pretty simple to create. All you need are

check boxes and a list of whatever the person needs in order to accomplish something.

The great thing about the checklists is they're a great way to make some money right away from your list.

If you have items on a checklist that a subscriber will need to purchase to get started, you can use affiliate links in your checklist.

The great thing about checklists are they're easy to create, helpful to your audience, and you can make some profit from them.

Deliver the checklist in the same way you would deliver a report or a chapter of an eBook.

Printables

Printables are documents that serve a specific purpose, they are useful to help others accomplish something specific, usually something physical. For example: bingo templates for a girly slumber party or notes for a child's lunch box.

For example: If your niche was in baby showers you can create a printable document for games that the subscriber can use at the baby shower.

You would deliver the printables in the same way you would deliver a report or a chapter of an eBook.

Printables may be a little more challenging to create if you're going to be incorporating images and lines. But it's a really great idea and is well worth it.

Make your printables fun and colorful, really get creative. Have small images or samples of what the printables will look like once printed to entice prospects to subscribe.

Printables are not necessary for every niche, but they can come in handy.

Email Course

You can create an email course or a 7-day boot camp for your email subscribers.

It's basically like dripping information over time.

First, find out what you want your email course to be about. Then decide what specific thing from the course you're going to go over in each email.

Your course can last as long as you want it to. The most popular are 5-7 days. Which means 5-7 emails sent automatically to your subscribers over time using auto responder messages via your email marketing software.

First, type out the course and then separate it into several different emails. Keep in mind that your course doesn't have to be super long, people actually prefer shorter emails.

Also, remember that each day of the course should have an actionable item that your subscriber can take. So leave them with a little bit of homework each day.

At the end of the course, your subscriber should know how to do something to completion.

To setup, create the course and send out automatic email messages each day. This process should be automated by using your email auto responder from your email service.

Video Course

A video course is similar to an email course but it's done with video. There are many options you can use to create video.

Keep in mind that you don't have to be in the video, you can take a video of your desktop screen.

If you decide that you don't need to be in the video because you're teaching how to do something online, you can use free services such as Jing and Screen-Cast-O-Matic to record your screen.

These services are free and allow you to record your screen and save the video as a file that you can upload to YouTube or into your media folder in WordPress.

You are able to use YouTube as a platform for your video course. Just upload your video to YouTube and have it as an unlisted video. An unlisted video is a video that cannot be seen by anyone just coming to your YouTube channel, it's only seen by people who are given the link.

If you go the YouTube unlisted video route, deliver the course by setting up auto responders with your email service in order for the videos to go out in the subscribers email one at a time each day.

You also have the option of uploading the videos in your WordPress back office and sending the file URL/link from WordPress in the email and setting up your autoresponder emails so the subscriber will get them in the right sequence.

Video

Instead of having a video course, you can just have one video that teaches someone how to do something and is appealing to your target market.

You can use YouTube and make the video unlisted. Then when the subscriber gets the email message that is sent immediately to them after they confirm they'll have access to the video.

Free Consultation

A free consultation is an option, but there's only one problem with this, it's not automated and you'll have to spend a lot of time figuring out schedules times and dates that you and that prospect can meet.

You can give a consultation through email too, but that can get overwhelming and take a while.

But the great side of this is that you can learn a lot about your target market, so this may be a good idea for an opt-in offer for those who want to do more research so they can create a product for their audience in the future.

Free consultations can also be done through Skype, free conference call, or Google Hangouts-- there are a lot of options.

You can use Google Calendars to let your prospects know when you're available and if they're available at the same time they'll be able to schedule something with you.

Make sure you ask them questions like what they're struggling with and problems they encounter so you can use this information at a later date to create value for your audience.

Audio

You can create an audio MP3 as your opt-in offer. The audio can be a recording that teaches your subscriber how to do something; it'll be sort of like a podcast.

Record an audio by using programs like Free Conference Call, Skype, Audacity for windows, and SoundCloud.

Then you can send your audio file in the email that is sent immediately to the subscriber after they confirm their subscription.

The Take Away

As you can see, you have many options on how to create your opt-in offer and ways to deliver it so your subscriber can download it instantly.

Do what's best for your target market. If your target market is consuming a lot of audio, consider creating an MP3. Or if they love to read, create an eBook.

Whatever you decide, make sure it's quality and relevant. Many people will not read, watch, and listen to what you give them.

This is because there are tons of offers out there and

people trying to collect email addresses just like you.

So it's critical that you stand out and offer something of value even if they never consume your product.

The truth is, people don't value free stuff. If they spend a little money, it gives them more incentive to actually see what the product is about.

But on the other hand, some people will open and consume your free gift, and when they do, you want to make sure you've provided them with value by teaching them how to do something or making their life more convenient in some way.

Please do not worry about people getting your opt-in

offer and then unsubscribing, unsubscribes happen to everyone. This can be a blessing in disguise because you don't want anyone on your list that just wants to take for free and then leave. You want customers that are quality and understanding.

People may also unsubscribe if they aren't your target market, and that's a good thing because you only want to market to your target market.

Chapter 3: Getting Traffic to Your Squeeze Page

Now that you have you're opt-in offer set up and ready to go. You need to start getting traffic to it.

A squeeze page is a page that you create with the intention to get the prospects email address and nothing else.

There should be nothing else on this page except information about your opt-in offer.

The box that prospects put their email address in should be visible without them having to scroll down the page.

To optimize your squeeze page, create a picture of what you're giving away, if at all possible. For example: show the eBook cover if you're giving away an eBook.

Make the words on the squeeze page enticing. Tell the prospect what to do. For example:

- download my FREE eBook

- get my FREE audio when you...

Do not use the words subscribe or newsletter. Those are words prospects don't like. It sounds like they'll be getting another sales message coming into their inbox.

People don't like the sound of a newsletter, they already have enough of those boring things.

The emails you'll be sending are email autoresponders that will help build relationships with your subscribers, not a newsletter on things they can learn just by going to your blog.

There are so many places to get traffic to your squeeze page. Here is a list of places to start:

- YouTube

- Facebook

- Twitter

- Pinterest

- Google +

- Slide Share

- Yahoo Answers

- Reddit

- Guest Posting

- Forums

- Facebook Groups

- Kindle Books

- Your Website

All of these are popular places that have high traffic, and will bring traffic to your squeeze page, and in turn, increase the amount of email subscribers on your list.

I suggest mastering one or two of these platforms at a time so you're not diluting your efforts.

Now I'm going to go into how to get traffic from each

particular platform.

YouTube

This is the best way to get traffic to your squeeze page because there are millions of videos viewed every single day on YouTube.

And many people are not on YouTube because they're too busy blogging. A lot of people are afraid to put themselves out there on video, this is where you can come in and take the lead.

There may be others creating videos in your niche, but believe me, there are many more trying to get traffic by creating blog posts or posting on Facebook instead.

So, it'll be easy for you to get email subscribers this way. Video is a way for you to build relationships with your prospects. They get to see you and learn from you. And they'll love it.

But keep in mind that you don't have to be in the videos, but you should at least have one video on your channel with your face so they can see what you look like and hear your voice.

In each video you create, tell people to check out your opt-in offer.

Also, have a link to your squeeze page as the first thing in your video description.

If they're getting quality content, they'll be happy to

subscribe.

Facebook

I'm a strong believer that social media sites like Facebook is a place to build relationships and not to sell or spam them with your opt-in offer. So if you're going to go the Facebook route make sure you're posting consistently on your page with other valuable content before asking for their email addresses.

If your posting every hour, mention your opt-in offer 2 times a day. If you're not posting every hour, only mention it once a day.

Facebook Ads are a great way to get subscribers. The

great thing about Facebook Ads is how you can break your advertising down to your target market. Create an ad for your target market that goes straight back to your squeeze page or an app in Facebook that collects name and emails.

You can also run a giveaway ad on Facebook where you're giving away something your target market would like, such as a t-shirt that says something cool. In order for them to enter to win the t-shirt, they'd have to enter their email address.

There are a lot of things you can do on Facebook to get subscribers without spamming.

Twitter

You can approach getting subscribers on twitter similar to the way you'd get them on Facebook.

I have my Facebook account linked to my Twitter account so when I post on Facebook it automatically posts on Twitter.

But if you don't a have similar setup, you can create content for your Twitter page and offer you're opt-in offer. Use hashtags with relevant keywords in order to get more eyes on your tweets.

Start building a community on Twitter and people will opt into your list.

Pinterest

Pinterest is another way you can get email subscribers.

It's a fast growing social media site and women love it.

Pinterest is a great way to drive traffic to anything, if you have an image of your opt-in offer that is appealing and you use hashtags to get more eyeballs on it you're very likely to get opt-ins.

Whatever content you post on Pinterest, you have the opportunity to link straight back to your squeeze page.

Google +

Google plus is very similar to Facebook but it doesn't have as much traffic. Just like Facebook post relevant content and then post about your opt-in offer every so often.

Slide Share

Slideshare is a social media site that hosts millions of PowerPoints that help solve people's problems.

Many people find content that was posted there by searching in Google to solve a problem they have.

Create PowerPoint presentations on Slideshare that helps out your target market, and at the end of the show make sure to mention your opt-in offer and a link over to your squeeze page.

Yahoo Answers

Yahoo Answers is a place where people all over the world ask questions. Type in a keyword that your target market would be asking questions about.

Go in and answer as many questions as you can to the best of your ability. You can leave a link back to your squeeze page.

Make sure you're very helpful so you can be voted as the best answer. This will get your rank high in Yahoo Answers.

Reddit

Reddit is a site where many people share content and

users can rate it up or down.

Share valuable content, and if you have your website for getting people to opt-in to your list, you'll get new subscribers.

The more traffic you get to your site the more chances you have of people opting in.

Guest Posting

Guest posting is when you go to sites that are popular in your niche, and that already have a large audience and guest posting on their site.

First, you have to get permission from the site owner. So make sure to email the owner to ask if you can do a guest post.

Your guest post should be very quality, and at the end of the post, you can put a link back to your squeeze page.

If the post is not quality the owner will not let you post it, and if they did let you post it prospects would not opt in.

Forums

Forums are online communities people go to help others and answer questions.

First, find a forum that has a lot of people from your target market. Then make sure you're very active and helping people in the forum.

Some forums allow you to have an about me page or links at the bottom of each post you make that goes back to your website.

If you're helping others in the forums out and telling them of the successes you've had they'll want to check you out.

Facebook Groups

The same thing goes for Facebook Groups as it does for Forums. Find relevant groups that have prospects in your target market, and offer value to them by answering questions.

Make sure not to spam your opt-in offer in these groups or you will get kicked out and or lose your credibility.

Kindle Books

Kindle books are a great way to get email subscribers while making some extra money on the side.

Create a book that is valuable and truly helps others and you will get email subscribers because they'll see that you have quality content.

Keep in mind that your soul purpose to is to get email subscribers, and not make money. So you may want to make this book permanently free or only $0.99. Get my free kindle creation course by visiting:

http://www.argenaolivis.com/freekindlecourse

Your Website

Make sure your website is optimized for getting email subscribers. Do this by using the plugin called "Add To Content", and add an opt-in form to the bottom of each page or post.

Also, make sure you add an opt-in form to your right sidebar.

Have a link to your squeeze page on the top of your navigation bar. Make sure that you're using every opportunity to collect names and emails for prospects that come to your website.

You can also use more aggressive by using tactics like pop-ups and light boxes.

If you haven't created a website yet, visit http://www.argenaolivis.com/website/ for a step by step tutorial on how to set it up.

The Takeaway

Use every opportunity you can to get people to your squeeze page without spamming.

The best practice is to create quality content and in turn, this will make people want to subscribe to see what else you have to offer.

Chapter 4: Setting Up Auto Responders

The great thing about email marketing is the fact that you can send out emails in your sleep.

You don't want to spend all of your time sending out emails. The great thing about using email software is the time it saves you.

In Aweber, you're able to set up auto responder messages. This means you can create emails once and put them in your autoresponder queue, and they'll be sent out to each person that subscribes in the order that you want them sent.

Each subscriber will get each email from the beginning of the sequence all the way to the end.

The first thing you want to do is to create a list for your target market. The emails you send to these subscribers will be relevant.

Create a series of emails that will be sent out to your list automatically. The best rule of thumb is about every 2 days. Every day is a bit much, every two days ensures that they don't forget about you.

Each message you send out should not be super long, it should just be long enough to get the point across.

When linking to your website to refer them to a blog post or page, make sure that the email is relevant to the content on that specific blog post or page.

Your email should have only one call to action. Do not confuse your subscriber by sending multiple links to different places in one email.

I recommend only linking to one specific destination.

Set up your email sequence in a way that makes sense. Only send out broadcasts when you have a new product that is launching or you have an announcement to make. You already have email auto responders being sent out, and subscribers don't want to get too many emails from you in one day.

In order to avoid emailing your subscribers twice in one day, have a set day that you send out autoresponders and broadcasts. For example: Have autoresponders sent out only on weekdays so you know it's safe to send a broadcast email on the weekends.

Broadcasts are emails that can be sent to your list immediately, you can also schedule broadcasts. They can be sent to your entire list no matter if they're a new subscriber or an old one.

Other Email Auto Responder Tips

If relevant, use the best content that you already have made for your autoresponders. It's likely that new subscribers haven't read all your blog posts or watched all your YouTube videos yet, so send them over to some of your best stuff.

When sharing a link with your audience, share the link very early in the email and also toward the middle and end (depending on how long the email is) to ensure that your catering to all your subscribers.

There will be impatient ones who like you to just get to the point and other ones who want to read the whole email before they decide if they want to click the link. Some people just want more information.

Again, when setting up your autoresponder series, it's important that you provide your subscribers with your best content. There's a lot of competition out there, so you want to make sure your subscribers look forward to email coming from you.

A rule of thumb is to think to yourself: "would I want this in my inbox?" before sending an email. Have a servant's heart, and always be looking for ways to help your audience, and you should be fine.

To increase open rates make sure to look up some catchy email headlines. My favorite place to get ideas is from magazines, they have the best headlines for their articles; so magazines is where I get a lot of my inspiration for email subject headlines.

The Takeaway

Don't overwhelm your list and have a clear call to action in each email. Automate your list by creating a series of emails that are sent out ever two days with relevant and quality content.

Chapter 5: Selling

Now the fun part. Selling to your list. There's a lot of thought that goes into selling to your list.

You want to make sure you're not alienating them and losing your credibility by recommending low-quality affiliate products that you haven't used yourself.

You have the option to create your own products and market them to your list, or to recommend affiliate products and earn a commission if they purchase the product through your affiliate link.

Only recommend affiliate products that you have used before or that you know for sure are quality.

This will just make things go a lot smoother. Because if a subscriber has a question about the product and you can't answer it from your own point of view-- that doesn't look very good.

When selling to your list you want to offer a range of products. This is because everyone won't buy everything you offer. Some people will buy all the products, some will by some, and some will buy none.

You're going to be setting up the products you want to promote in auto responder messages.

Separate Lists

The best way to find out if a subscriber is interested in a particular product is to put them on a separate list, do this by creating a new list and sending a link to another free opt-in offer in the email.

If they subscribe, this confirms that they're interested in the particular subject. So you can set up a series of autoresponders around the product.

Selling Directly

When you feel you have provided enough value to your list, promote your product or the affiliate product. Don't be shy, it's time to be paid back for all the value you've given them and there's nothing wrong with that.

The previous emails your subscribers received should have been very quality and should have added value. If they know you put out quality content, then they'll be comfortable buying from you and taking your word that the product can help them.

The first product you promote should be valued between $1-$7. You don't want to start off selling a very expensive product.

The second product you offer, a few emails later, can be between $7-$40.

You just keep going up in price with every offer.

You don't have to do it this way, but it's the way many internet marketers are doing it. It's called upselling.

When you're promoting a product make sure it links back to a high converting sales page.

Affiliate Marketing

Make sure to brush up on your affiliate marketing skills. Do research on the product to make sure that it's valuable and will get your subscribers results.

Many affiliate programs come with email templates that you can send to your subscribers, some even have training on how to sell the products. Go with trusted sources like Clickbank, Share A Sale, Commission Junction, and JVzoo when searching for affiliate products to promote.

If you really want to go above and beyond, create bonuses for when subscribers buy through your affiliate link. You can also create tutorials and product reviews; show your subscribers that you actually use the product, share the results you've gotten with it.

The Takeaway

Don't be afraid to sell. Selling helps people to take action. A lot of people take free information for granted and don't use it. Sometimes a paid product is just what they need in order to get serious.

Chapter 6: Building Relationships

The most important thing you want to make sure you're doing with your email list is building relationships.

You can do this by making sure you're keeping in touch with your list. This is why I recommend setting up auto responders so they'll remember who you are.

Action Step: Make sure to set up at least 10 auto responders to get started for each of your email lists.

If you personalize the email enough, you'll get a lot of responses. Make sure to reply to each one. People sometimes don't know it's an autoresponder but make sure you're replying back. This could be a potential long term fan that may purchase all of your products in the future that is reaching out to you.

Create a survey with a free service called Survey Monkey and send it out to your list. Ask questions to find out more of what they want and what kind of products they're willing to pay for.

The best question to ask in one of your earlier auto responders is: "what are you struggling with." Then you can create content, products, and solutions to solve these problems.

Tell stories in your emails so your subscribers can get to know you. Open up to them.

Also, make sure to build credibility so they can see why you're worth listening to.

You can build credibility by telling them the results you received by using a particular method you're introducing, etc.

Invite them to like your Facebook fan page in one of the earlier messages, let them know you want to get to know them better.

Consider sending "subscriber only" emails, and make it known to your subscribers when it's exclusive so they can feel special and appreciated.

Give them freebies when you can, and just be obsessed with sharing all you have with them and not holding anything back, want the best for them.

When sending an email, pretend like you're writing it to a friend or family member, put your personality into it. Don't capitalize your email subject headlines, be as natural as possible.

One of the best ways to connect is to create videos, your subscribers want to see and hear you; they want to know you're real. Don't hide behind your emails and blog posts.

The Takeaway

Building relationships with your email list by telling stories, establishing credibility and sending them quality content will decrease you're unsubscribe rate and increase the trust with your audience.

What you want to keep in mind when writing a new email is not to be aggressive. Act as if you're writing it to a friend. Just be yourself and offer them help and guidance.

Conclusion

Thank you again for reading *Email Marketing Machine*. Make sure to set up your machine as soon as possible to create a valuable business asset and a community of people who help support you and your business.

I hope this book was able to help you to build relationships, traffic and make money with your email list.

The next step is to take action on the tips and information provided. Set up your squeeze page, get traffic to it, set up your auto responders and your machine will be well oiled!

Finally, if you enjoyed this book, then I'd like to ask you

for a favor, would you be kind enough to leave a review

for this book on Amazon? It'd be greatly appreciated!

Your reviews help others to find the book, and it also

gives me feedback on what I can improve on or lets me

know what I did well.

Thank you and good luck!

Preview of 'How To Make Money Online Fast'

Chapter 1: Kindle Publishing

Wow, where do I begin? You should know that I started my online journey in 2012. I was in college and looking for a way to make some extra money online.

That's when I came across website creation. While researching how to create a website on YouTube I was shocked to find that there were people making tons of money online.

That's when I started going from "I want to make money online" to "I want to create an online business."

As the story goes, I started reading business books, buying courses, and of course building websites.

Many of the websites I built failed and never made a profit. Then everything changed, I decided I didn't want to work a job, I wanted to be an entrepreneur full time.

So I started to really focus on making an income online. I purchased two courses that then changed my life.

I started taking massive action and, now I'm here, making a decent income online and writing this book to you-- the person who also has dreams of making their first dollar online.

Believe me, this stuff really works. You just have to change your mindset and really do the work.

None of these strategies work without work. You may find yourself up late and up early, or sacrificing your TV time to try to make this work.

Whatever you do, if you truly want to make it you have to put in the time and you have to want it bad enough.

I found that Kindle Publishing by far the simplest method of making money online. This is because Amazon is the number one website that people shop.

So if you know what you're doing, you can truly clean up on Amazon.

How To Create A Kindle Book

The "how to" of creating a kindle book is pretty simple; optimizing it so that it can be found is the harder part.

Yes, Amazon has a lot of customers, but it also has a lot of authors. More and more people are publishing Kindle books every single day and every day the marketplace is becoming more saturated.

It's one of those things where you better get in when you can.

Step 1: Decide what market or niche that you want to write your book in. You have options to write nonfiction books, fiction books, erotica, and children's books.

It should be a niche you're familiar with. If you do decide to write a book in a niche you're not familiar with, make sure to do the proper research in order to create a quality book.

It's important that the niche that you write your book in is profitable.

If you decide to write a nonfiction book, look up the keyword that you want to target in the Amazon Kindle store. If you see books on the first page for the keyword and has rank under 100,000 then it's a profitable niche.

Typically books with an Amazon sales rank lower than 100,000 are making $30+ a month.

Step 2: Create a title for your book. When writing a nonfiction book use the keywords from the niche you've chosen. Your title should have relevant keywords in it so it can be found easily in the kindle store.

Step 3: Open up a writing document of your choice and type out your book.

Depending on how familiar you are with the subject, you can finish your book in a day. I typically try to write for 2 hours a day, so I can finish books in about 3-7 days.

If you're writing a children's book you will have to hire an illustrator. You can find low priced illustrators by going to www.fiverr.com.

Your book does not have to be long, but it does have to be quality if you truly want to make sales. Bad reviews can slow down or eliminate your sales.

Unless it's a children's book, your book should be 15 or more pages.

You can find a template online by Googling kindle templates if you want to use a template to guide your writing.

Your nonfiction book should include an introduction, 4-6 chapters, and a conclusion.

Step 4: Upload your book to KDP. Go to

www.kdp.amazon.com and if you haven't done so yet, open up a KDP account.

Add all the necessary information into KDP. The whole process is pretty self-explanatory, so you'll be able to enter the necessary information.

Step 5: Design your cover using the Kindle Cover Creator. The Kindle Cover Creator is a free software by Amazon that you can use to create your book covers. They give you free templates, it's really cool.

If you're creative and design well, this too will be very beneficial to you. If not, I suggest going to www.fiverr.com and ordering your cover for only $5.

Then you're finished. The process gets easier as you

continue to create more and more books.

If your book is not selling, consider this:

- the niche may be too competitive

- you're not using the correct keywords

- you have a lot of bad reviews

- your cover is not attractive enough

- your book is not in the correct categories or the categories are too competitive

There are many factors that go into rather or not your book sells. Make sure you enroll your book in the KDP select program in order to have a free promotion for your book.

These free promotions are for 5 days every three months. When a lot of people download your book it will help your book rank for its keywords.

So now the thing to do is take action! Use this guide and start creating your kindle book today. The sooner you get it up, the faster you make money online!

Discover more ways to promote your kindle book by taking my video course on how to create and market your first kindle book:

http://www.argenaolivis.com/freekindlecourse

Click here to check out the rest of How To Make Money Online on Amazon.

Check Out My Other Books

Below you'll find some of my other popular books that are popular on Amazon and Kindle as well. Alternatively, you can visit my author page on Amazon to see other work done by me.

Affiliate Marketing: How To Make Money With Other People's Products

Information Products: How To Create and Make Money With Information

How To Make Money Online Fast: Step By Step Instructions On How To Work From Home Using Proven Internet Marketing Strategies

Online Business Mindset: Personal Development & Confidence Building For Internet Marketers

Kindle Publishing Back End: Guide To Creating A Real Business With Kindle Publishing

BONUS: Squeeze Page Traffic Machine Video + Bonus Report [FREE]

Get access to my newest course **Squeeze Page Traffic Machine** absolutely free. Learn how to drive targeted traffic to your squeeze using these simple tactics.

Visit <u>www.argenaolivis.com/squeezepagetraffic</u> for Access

www.ingramcontent.com/pod-product-compliance
Lightning Source LLC
Chambersburg PA
CBHW070831180526
45168CB00002B/806